ALLISON HILL

Urban Decay: Deprivation in the Shadow of Prosperity

by

Drs. Karen and Dierich Kaiser

To the love of our life:
Ryan Kaiser.

TABLE OF CONTENTS

ALLISON HILL   5

THE GOOD PEOPLE OF THE SUBURBS   12

INJUSTICE   13

DEPRIVATION IN THE SHADOW OF PROSPERITY   14

DERRY STREET CHURCH   19

"YOU REALLY LIVE THERE?"   21

LUCY   23

BLIGHT   24

LOST IN AMERICA   27

MAYOR   29

ALLISON HILL

Anything neglected will ultimately decay.

Such is the state of the once illustrious Allison Hill.

Grand homes on top of a hill.

Victorian, Queen Anne, Neo-Classical still.

Now old.

They were young when they came.

Proud and conscientious.

The good people of Allison Hill.

Industries thrived and so did they.

Things change, people age, jobs go away.

People follow.

Forgotten, still proud.

They watched the neighborhood erode and decay.

Reasons aplenty.

Corruption, ineptness, greed.

Leadership looked the other way and into their own pocket.

Those who could, fled to the new and cast the old away.

Few stood by what they built,

Allison Hill.

THE GOOD PEOPLE OF THE SUBURBS

They arrive every morning.

Only to leave…

When the sun sets.

When the snow falls.

When the storms arrive.

They go.

Suggesting what?

No!

It's a shake down.

Use the City up!

Take the money.

Leave nothing to shelter what they have left behind.

The good people of the suburbs?

INJUSTICE

It is painful to witness injustice.

That leaves such suffering in its wake.

People are starving.

It is cold!

Babies don't have shoes.

Privatization.

Blight.

So the few can have more.

Ignore more.

Blame more.

Who will take responsibility?

DEPRIVATION IN THE SHADOW OF PROSPERITY

Winners and losers.

Both must exist?

How do we know we have won,

unless someone has lost.

So we cast blame.

We separate from THEM.

Deprivation in the shadow of prosperity.

It's ironic.

That a hill sits in the shadows?

Do you have enough yet?

How much do you need?

DERRY STREET CHURCH

Bring, love, hope and meaning as Christ directs.

So few left.

Try to be!

The hands of the Almighty.

Witness, but do not fall to despair!

Source of joy and hope.

The basics.

Food and clothing and wellness.

Politics interrupts.

Greed hovers nearby.

The Pastor endures.

Leads.

Take responsibility where government has failed!

"YOU REALLY LIVE THERE?"

He asked.

With other like-minded.

Ignorant.

Self-righteous.

We needed this!

To see, to witness.

To experience the indifference first hand.

We didn't know.

Now, we do.

What do we do?

We are not brave.

Doing nothing is not an option.

Becoming like them is an abomination.

How do we fit in?

MPA, PHD, MD, MS, MED, BS, BA.

Didn't prepare us for this.

Pick up the trash!

Hand out the food and clothing.

Pay tithes.

Provide therapy, medication.

Write about what we see?

LUCY

Run, jump and play.

Smile, be polite, share.

Take care of your brother and sister.

You provide a safe place.

Warmth.

Nutritious meals.

A helping hand and a shoulder to lean on.

Tutoring for those who will.

Soft spoken, but firm,

A mother to many.

Safe haven.

BLIGHT

Are you blind?

Do you see it?

How can you not?

It is here!

Trash blowing.

Houses crumbling,

Even the streets!

Strays -- animals, people…

Danger from those who take advantage of the neglect.

Move in and frighten the vulnerable!

The disabled, the poor, the weary…

They cannot escape.

They cannot fight the blight.

LOST IN AMERICA

Is it possible?

To live your entire life,

believing you are an American.

Only to find out that you are not.

You are an illegal immigrant.

You thought you knew your Country.

You thought you knew your name.

You don't know either.

You are lost in America!

You can not work.

You do not qualify for benefits.

They want you out!

Gone!

Erased!

But you have no Country.

No home.

So you stay,

Lost in America.

MAYOR

You go girl!

They call you angry, hostile, bitter...

Perhaps, you are.

You should be!

We all should be!

They should call you brave warrior.

You fight for your heritage, the City you remember.

A child of Harrisburg.

A child of Allison Hill.